BIG BEASTS
Elephant

Stephanie Turnbull

Published by Smart Apple Media
P.O. Box 1329
Mankato, MN 56002

Printed in the United States of America,
at Corporate Graphics in North Mankato, Minnesota.

Designed by Helen James
Edited by Mary-Jane Wilkins

Library of Congress Cataloging-in-Publication Data

Turnbull, Stephanie.
 Elephant / Steph Turnbull.
    p. cm. -- (Big beasts)
 Includes index.
 Summary: "An introduction on elephants, the big beasts of Asian
and African grasslands. Describes how elephants move, find food,
communicate, and care for their young. Also mentions the different
kinds of elephants and their differences"--Provided by publisher.
 ISBN 978-1-59920-833-6 (hardcover, library bound)
 1. Elephants--Juvenile literature. I. Title.
 QL737.P98T866 2013
 599.67--dc23
                        2012004112

Photo acknowledgements
l = left, r = right, t = top, b = bottom
page 1 Martin Vrlik/Shutterstock; 3 Pal Teravagimov/Shutterstock;
4l Four Oaks, r Uryadnikov Sergey/both Shutterstock; 5 Eric
Isselée/Shutterstock; 6 Johan Swanepoel/Shutterstock; 7 Sean
Nel/Shutterstock; 8l Kitch Bain/Shutterstock; 8-9 iStockphoto/
Thinkstock; 10 iStockphoto/Thinkstock; 11 Anan Kaewkhammul/
Shutterstock; 12 iStockphoto/Thinkstock; 13 Four Oaks/
Shutterstock; 14 iStockphoto/Thinkstock; 15 Jupiterimages/
Thinkstock; 16 Four Oaks/Shutterstock; 17 Four Oaks/
Shutterstock; 18 Anke van Wyk/Shutterstock; 19 iStockphoto/
Thinkstock; 20 Jupiterimages/Thinkstock; 21 Photodisc/
Thinkstock; 22l Helen Cingisiz, r Laschon Maximilian, b Frogstar;
23tl higyou, tr Morphart, br mihalec/all Shutterstock
Cover Talvi/Shutterstock

DAD0503
042012
9 8 7 6 5 4 3 2 1

Contents

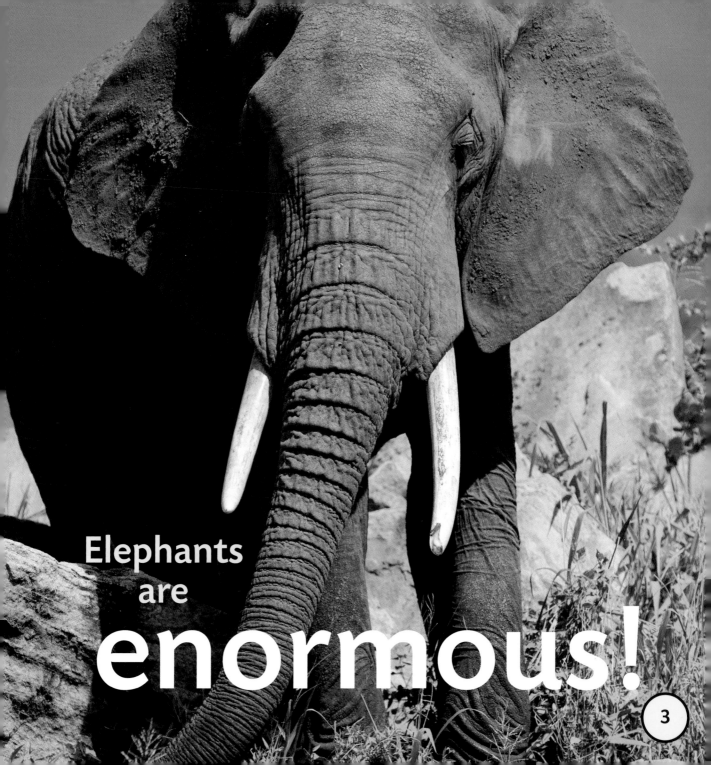

Elephants
are
enormous!

Spot the Difference

There are three types of elephants.

African bush elephants have long, curved tusks and huge ears.

African forest elephants are smaller, and have rounder ears.

Asian elephants have small ears and a bulging forehead.

Elephants are the biggest land animals in the world.

Follow the Leader

Female elephants live in big family groups. The oldest is the leader.

Male elephants, called bulls, live alone or in small groups.

On the Move

Elephants spend the day searching for food in the flat, grassy lands where they live.

Sometimes they wade across rivers.

They have good memories, so they remember where to go.

Munch, Munch

Elephants eat a lot. They love plants.

An elephant uses its strong trunk to pull leaves and bark off trees or grab grass and fruit...

...then it crams the food into its mouth.

11

Giant
Tusks

Tusks are
enormous
front teeth.

Each tusk weighs much more than you.

Elephants use their sharp tusks to move things, dig for tasty roots, or fight.

Staying Cool

Elephants get very hot in the sun.

They flap their ears to lose heat or suck water up their trunk and blast it out like a shower.

Mud keeps elephants cool and
protects their skin from burning.

Big Babies

A baby elephant is called a calf.

Calves are weak and wobbly
at first. They stay close to
their mom and drink her milk.

Mothers take good care of their calves.

Growing Up

Calves love playing. They splash in water, roll in mud and wrestle with other calves.

They learn to use their trunks and find food.
Soon they will be able to look after themselves.

Watch Out!

Animals such as lions and tigers may attack calves.

If they see an enemy, elephants flap their ears, stamp their feet and blow air through their trunk to say, "GO AWAY!"

Then they **charge!**

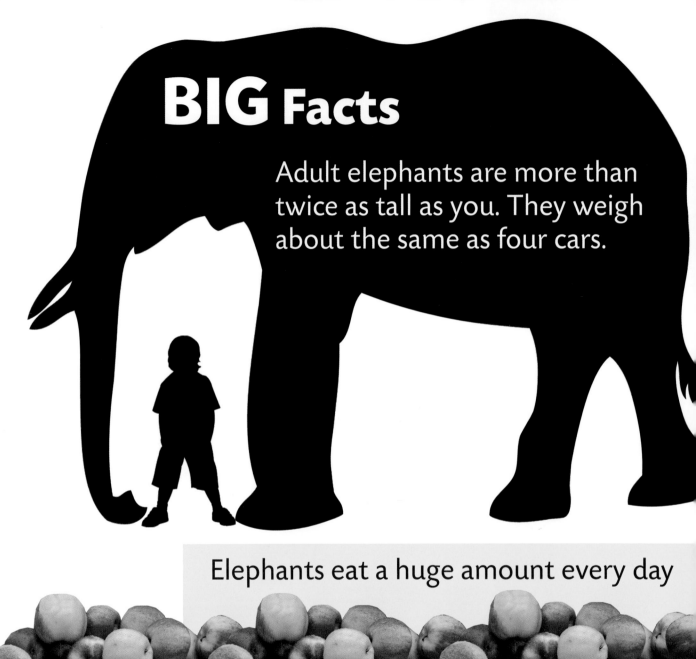

BIG Facts

Adult elephants are more than twice as tall as you. They weigh about the same as four cars.

Elephants eat a huge amount every day

Elephants can drink more than two bathtubs of water a day.

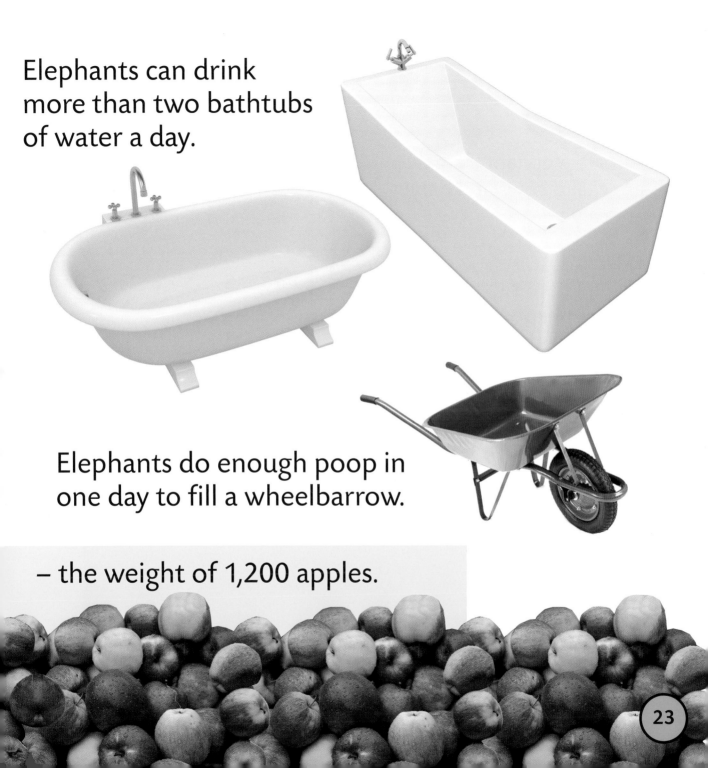

Elephants do enough poop in one day to fill a wheelbarrow.

– the weight of 1,200 apples.

Useful Words

bull
A male elephant. Females are called cows and babies are calves.

trunk
An elephant's long nose. The elephant uses it to hold and move things, and to smell, suck and blow.

tusks
Long, hard teeth.

Web Link

Go to this website to read all about elephants and see calves playing:
http://www.nationalgeographic.com/kids/animals/creaturefeature/african-elephant